THE
BEANZ
BOOK

THE
BEANZ
BOOK

INTRODUCTION

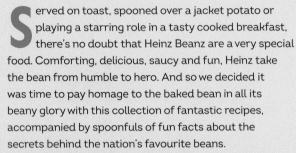

Served on toast, spooned over a jacket potato or playing a starring role in a tasty cooked breakfast, there's no doubt that Heinz Beanz are a very special food. Comforting, delicious, saucy and fun, Heinz take the bean from humble to hero. And so we decided it was time to pay homage to the baked bean in all its beany glory with this collection of fantastic recipes, accompanied by spoonfuls of fun facts about the secrets behind the nation's favourite beans.

Whether you want to add extra flavour to a veggie stew or recreate the iconic Beanz Pizza, the recipes in this book will show you dozens of new and fun ways to use Heinz Beanz in your kitchen, while the amazing stories and vintage ads will take you on a tasty trip down memory lane.

So pull up a chair, pop on the kettle, and let's dive in.

A BRIEF HISTORY OF HEINZ BEANZ

In 1869, the 25-year-old Henry John Heinz started bottling and selling horseradish sauce made according to his mother's recipe. Although this business didn't last, by 1876 Henry had teamed up with his brother John and cousin Frederick, and the trio were selling tomato ketchup.

In 1886, Henry started selling his products in the UK, too, and the Heinz repertoire quickly expanded to include a huge range of delicious foods, including pickles, mustards, preserves – and, in 1895, baked beans.

By 1901, Heinz Baked Beans were being exported to the UK, and were originally sold in Fortnum & Mason as a delicacy costing 9d per can (£2.15 in today's money). They quickly became a national favourite, and in 1928 the first can of British-manufactured Heinz Baked Beans was produced in the new Heinz factory in Harlesden, London.

During the Second World War, when food shortages hit and rationing became necessary, the Ministry of Food declared Heinz Baked Beans an 'essential food'. We couldn't agree more!

Heinz was granted the Royal Warrant in 1951, an honour the company still holds today, and 1959 saw the opening of a new Heinz factory in Kitt Green, Wigan, the largest food factory in Europe.

In 2004, Heinz changed the spelling to Heinz Baked Beanz in honour of the classic 1960s advertising slogan 'Beanz Meanz Heinz' – and a few years later, in 2008, the name was simplified to Heinz Beanz. The beans that we all know and love, however, have stayed the same, and a staggering 1.5 million cans are sold in the UK every day.

Henry John Heinz starts his business selling bottles of horseradish sauce.

Heinz products are launched in the UK and sold at Fortnum & Mason.

Heinz Baked Beans are exported to the UK and quickly become a firm favourite.

The Ministry of Food declares Heinz Baked Beans an 'essential food' as part of rationing in the Second World War.

The first Heinz TV advert airs on ITV.

| 1869 | 1876 | 1886 | 1895 | 1901 | 1928 | 1941 -48 | 1951 | 1955 | 1959 |

Heinz Tomato Ketchup launches in the US.

Canned baked beans are first produced by the Heinz company in Pittsburgh.

The first can of British-manufactured Heinz Baked Beans is produced at the Heinz factory in Harlesden, London.

Heinz is granted the Royal Warrant.

A new Heinz factory is opened in Kitt Green, Wigan, becoming the largest food factory in Europe. It remains one of the biggest today and produces more than 1 billion cans every year.

HEINZ BEANZ TIMELINE

The now iconic 'Beanz Meanz Heinz' slogan is created.

Heinz Baked Beans are now exported to 60 countries worldwide.

Heinz launches a new Mean Beanz range, with Mexican, Sweet Chilli and Smoky BBQ flavours.

Heinz Five Beanz are launched, along with a range of tasty Flavoured Beanz.

After many decades of Beanzy goodness, Heinz Beanz remain a storecupboard essential and huge family favourite, with more than 540 million cans sold in the UK every year.

1967 1986 1990 2004 2005 2008 2012 2019 TODAY

Heinz celebrates 100 successful years in the UK.

Heinz changes the name to Heinz Baked Beanz, adopting the 'z' spelling in honour of the famous 'Beanz Meanz Heinz' slogan.

The name changes once more, to Heinz Beanz: simple and delicious, just like the beans!

To celebrate 150 years of Heinz, a Heinz Beanz museum is opened in London.

ULTIMATE VEGGIE BREAKFAST

VEGETARIAN
PREP 5 MINUTES
COOK 20 MINUTES

1 medium free-range egg

1 tbsp whole milk

2 tsp za'atar (optional)

salt and pepper

2½ tbsp olive oil

2 slices of white bread

2 portobello mushrooms, sliced

1 fat garlic clove, crushed

150g cherry tomatoes, halved

100g kale

200g tin Heinz Beanz

½ tsp smoked paprika

6 slices of halloumi

Preheat the oven to 120°C/100°C fan/gas mark ½.

In a bowl, whisk together the egg and milk, along with the za'atar, if using, and plenty of seasoning.

Heat 1 tablespoon of the oil in a large non-stick frying pan over a medium heat. Dip the bread slices into the egg mixture to coat, then lay them in the pan. Cook for 1–2 minutes on each side until crisp and golden. Transfer to a roasting tray and put in the oven to keep warm.

Briefly wash the frying pan, then place it over a high heat. Add another 1 tablespoon of oil. Add the mushrooms and fry, stirring, for 10 minutes until golden and crisp. Add the garlic and cook for 30 seconds, then season. Transfer to the roasting tray along with the French toast and keep warm.

Reduce the heat to medium and add the remaining oil to the pan. Add the tomatoes and kale and stir. At the same time, heat the beans in a small saucepan over a medium heat for 2–3 minutes until warmed through.

Stir the paprika into the kale and tomatoes, then push them to one side of the pan. Increase the heat to high and fry the halloumi slices in the other half of the pan for 1 minute on each side until crisp.

Once everything is ready, arrange the ultimate veggie breakfast on plates and serve.

BEANZ-IN-A-HOLE
SANDWICH

PREP 5 MINUTES
COOK 15 MINUTES

6 back bacon rashers (we like
smoked)

415g tin Heinz Beanz

2–3 tsp hot sauce (we like
sriracha) (optional)

4 slices of white bread

20g butter

HP Sauce or Heinz Tomato
Ketchup, to serve

Preheat the oven to 120°C/100°C fan/gas mark ½.

Lay out the bacon rashers in a dry non-stick frying pan over a high heat and fry for 2–3 minutes on each side, depending on how crispy you like your bacon. Transfer to a roasting tray and keep warm in the oven.

Tip the beans into a small saucepan over a medium heat. Add the hot sauce, if using, and cook for 3–4 minutes, stirring occasionally, until heated through.

Meanwhile, use a cookie cutter or the bottom of the bean tin to cut a hole out of the centre of two of the bread slices, keeping the remaining bread slices whole.

Put the bacon pan back over a medium–high heat (don't wash it in between, you want the bacon flavour!). Add the butter to melt, then lay all four bread slices in the pan. Fry for a minute or so on each side until crisp.

Take out two plates and place a whole bread slice on each one. Top each with 3 bacon rashers, then place the holey bread on top. Pour the beans into the holes and serve with HP Sauce or ketchup for extra sauciness!

CORN MUFFINS

VEGETARIAN OPTION
PREP 15 MINUTES
COOK 20 MINUTES

1 medium free-range egg
100ml whole milk
salt and pepper
175g self-raising flour
50g butter, melted
200g tin Heinz Beanz
200g tin sweetcorn, drained
1 tsp smoked paprika
zest of 1 lime
8 pickled jalapeño slices,
    chopped
75g Manchego or extra-
    mature Cheddar, coarsely
    grated

*You will need a 12-hole muffin
tray and 12 muffin cases.*

Preheat the oven to 180°C/160°C fan/gas mark 4 and line a 12-hole muffin tray with muffin cases.

Crack the egg into a jug and add the milk, then whisk well with a fork to combine. Season with salt and pepper.

Put the flour in a large bowl and make a well in the centre. Pour in the egg mixture, followed by the melted butter. Beat to form a smooth batter, then add the beans, sweetcorn, paprika, lime zest, pickled jalapeños and 50g of the cheese. Season with a pinch of salt and fold together to combine.

Divide the muffin batter between the cases, then sprinkle the remaining cheese over the top. Bake in the centre of the oven for 15–20 minutes until the muffins are puffed up and golden brown.

Serve warm or cold.

The muffins will keep for up to 2 days in an airtight container.

HOW ARE HEINZ
BEANZ MADE?

The small white beans used to make Heinz Beanz are haricot beans, also known as navy beans. Every year, more than 50,000 tonnes of haricot beans are shipped from North America to Liverpool, from where they are delivered to the Heinz factory in Wigan in two-tonne bags. An amazing 1,000 tonnes of these dried beans are used in the Heinz factory every week.

The beans are blanched, then sealed in tins with the special Heinz sauce. This rich tomato sauce is made from Mediterranean-grown tomatoes and a secret mix of spices that gives Heinz Beanz their distinctive flavour. The spice mix comes to the factory in bags marked with numbers rather than labels to ensure the precise ingredients remain secret. In fact, only four people in the whole world know the exact ingredients!

The sealed cans are then placed in huge pressure cookers to cook the beans and thicken the sauce – so the beans are actually cooked inside the can! Then they're ready to be labelled and delivered to the shops. The whole process, from haricot bean to a sealed, labelled tin, takes 90 minutes.

FULL ENGLISH FRITTATA

PREP 5 MINUTES
COOK 35 MINUTES

1 tsp olive oil
8 frozen hash browns
8 good-quality chipolata
  sausages
200g cherry tomatoes, left
  whole
8 streaky bacon rashers
8 medium free-range eggs
salt and pepper
415g tin Heinz Beanz
Heinz Tomato Ketchup and/or
  HP Sauce, to serve

Preheat the oven to 220°C/200°C fan/gas mark 7. Use the oil to lightly grease a 20 x 30cm roasting tin, then line it with baking paper.

Tip the frozen hash browns into the oiled tin. Roast for 5 minutes, then remove from the oven and add the chipolatas and cherry tomatoes to the tin. Return to the oven and bake for a further 10 minutes, then remove from the oven once more. Flip the hash browns and chipolatas, then lay the bacon rashers in the tin. Return to the oven and roast for a final 5 minutes until everything is cooked through.

Meanwhile, crack the eggs into a large jug. Whisk well with a fork, then season generously with salt and pepper.

Once everything is cooked, remove the roasting tin from the oven and carefully stir the beans into the tin, then pour in the beaten eggs.

Reduce the oven temperature to 180°C/160°C fan/gas mark 4, and bake the frittata for 15 minutes until the eggs are just set, and the whole thing is puffed up and golden brown.

Cut the frittata into four rectangles, and serve with tomato ketchup and/or HP Sauce.

ROOT VEGETABLE STEW WITH CHEDDAR DUMPLINGS

VEGETARIAN
PREP 15 MINUTES
COOK 50 MINUTES

3 tbsp olive oil

1 red onion, cut into 8 wedges

1 small butternut squash, peeled and cut into medium chunks

4 parsnips, peeled and cut into medium chunks

4 carrots, peeled and cut into medium chunks

salt and pepper

3 fat garlic cloves, crushed

2 x 415g tins Heinz Beanz

500ml vegetable stock

2 tsp yeast extract

For the dumplings

175g self-raising flour, plus extra for dusting

½ tsp baking powder

20g cold butter, diced

75ml whole milk

100g extra-mature Cheddar cheese, finely grated

handful of mixed herbs, finely chopped (we like parsley and chives)

Preheat the oven to 200°C/180°C fan/gas mark 6.

Heat the oil in your largest casserole pot over a medium-high heat. Add the onion, squash, parsnips and carrots, along with a pinch of salt. Cook, stirring regularly, for 5 minutes until the onion wedges begin to collapse.

Add the garlic and cook for 30 seconds more, then add the beans and vegetable stock. Give everything a good mix, then add the yeast extract. Bring to the boil, then reduce the heat to medium and leave to bubble away for 20 minutes until the vegetables are cooked through.

When the stew has about 5 minutes left to cook, make the dumplings. Sift the flour and baking powder into a large bowl. Add the butter, along with a pinch of salt, then use clean fingers to rub it all together until the mixture has a sandy texture. Pour in the milk, then add the Cheddar and mixed herbs. Bring everything together into a soft dough. Tip the dough out on to a lightly floured surface. Roll it into a rough sausage shape, then cut into 8 equal-sized pieces.

Season the stew to taste, then place the dumplings on top. Transfer to the oven and cook, uncovered, for 15–20 minutes until the dumplings are golden and cooked through. To serve, place the pot on a heatproof mat on the table for people to help themselves.

BEANZ FACTS

A lot of people think the first automated production line was Henry Ford's Model T assembly line, but Heinz actually got there first with the baked beans assembly line at their Pittsburgh factory.

Before it can become a Heinz Baked Bean, every single bean has to be tested by a special laser that checks its colour and size. If it passes the laser beam test, the bean can go for canning.

There are about **465** beans in a standard 415g tin.

MINESTRONE WITH PESTO CROUTONS

VEGETARIAN OPTION
PREP 15 MINUTES
COOK 35 MINUTES

3 tbsp olive oil

1 large onion, finely chopped

2 carrots, peeled and finely
chopped

2 celery stalks, finely chopped

salt and pepper

4 garlic cloves, crushed

1 tsp dried chilli flakes
(optional)

400g tin chopped tomatoes

415g tin Heinz Beanz

1 litre chicken or vegetable
stock

50g Parmesan or vegetarian
alternative, rind cut off and
cheese finely grated

3 slices of crusty white bread,
cut into large croutons (we
like ciabatta)

1 large head of broccoli, cut
into small florets and stalk
roughly chopped

3 tbsp basil pesto (check the
label if you're veggie)

½ small Savoy cabbage, very
finely sliced

Preheat the oven to 200°C/180°C fan/gas mark 6.

Heat 2 tablespoons of the olive oil in your largest saucepan over a medium heat. Add the onion, carrots and celery, along with a pinch of salt. Cook, stirring occasionally, for 8–10 minutes until coloured but not softened. Add the garlic and chilli flakes, if using, and cook for 30 seconds.

Add the chopped tomatoes, beans and stock, along with the cheese rind. Bring to a simmer.

Toss the bread croutons in the remaining oil and season. Spread out on a roasting tray in a single layer so that they cook evenly. Transfer to the oven and bake for 6 minutes.

Meanwhile, add the broccoli to the soup, then leave it to bubble away while the croutons bake.

After 6 minutes, remove the croutons from the oven and dollop the pesto into the roasting tray. Toss so that each crouton gets coated in pesto, then return to the oven for 3–4 minutes until golden and crisp. Set aside.

Add the cabbage to the soup and stir. Cook for another 3–4 minutes until the cabbage is wilted and soft, then season the minestrone to taste.

Fish out the cheese rind, then ladle the soup into four bowls and top with the grated cheese and pesto croutons to serve.

SPANISH-STYLE BAKED EGGS

PREP 5 MINUTES
COOK 20 MINUTES

1 tbsp olive oil
110g chorizo, peeled and sliced
2 roasted red peppers from a
   jar, drained and sliced
415g tin Heinz Beanz
2 tsp sherry vinegar
50g pitted green olives, sliced
salt and pepper
4 medium free-range eggs

For the rocket salad
30g rocket
1 tbsp olive oil
1 tsp sherry vinegar
50g Manchego, peeled into
   shavings

Preheat the oven to 200°C/180°C fan/gas mark 6.

Heat the olive oil in a large frying pan over a high heat. Add the chorizo and fry, stirring regularly, for 5-6 minutes until crisp. Now add the peppers, beans, sherry vinegar and green olives. Give everything a good mix, bring to a simmer, then season to taste.

Divide the chorizo and pepper mixture between two small baking dishes. Crack two eggs into each dish, then sprinkle over some salt and pepper.

Place the baking dishes on a roasting tray and bake for 8-12 minutes until the eggs are just cooked with a jammy yolk centre.

Meanwhile, make the rocket salad. In a bowl, mix the rocket with the olive oil and sherry vinegar. Add the Manchego shavings and toss to combine.

When everything is ready, serve the baked eggs alongside the rocket salad.

THE EVOLUTION OF THE HEINZ BEANZ TIN

1901

The year when Heinz first imported baked beans to the UK to sell at Fortnum & Mason.

PRE-1928

Already this early label has familiar elements.

1928

The first Heinz Baked Beans label design to come from the Heinz Harlesden factory in London.

1952

This was the design on Heinz Baked Beans tins when Queen Elizabeth II came to the throne. It was recreated in 2012 at Fortnum & Mason to celebrate her Diamond Jubilee.

2008

Heinz Baked Beanz becomes Heinz Beanz.

2013

Created as part of the Selfridges 'No Noise' campaign.

2017

Marking 50 years of Beanz Meanz Heinz.

1959

This is what the Heinz Baked Beans labels would have looked like in 1959, when Kitt Green factory opened. This label design was recreated as a limited edition in 2019 to celebrate Kitt Green's 60th anniversary.

MODERN

The more modern Heinz Baked Beans can.

2004

Heinz Baked Beans becomes Heinz Baked Beanz.

2007

Created to celebrate 300 years of Fortnum & Mason.

2019

Limited edition tins celebrating 150 years of Heinz.

CURRENT

The current Heinz Beanz tin.

CHEESY CROQUETTES

VEGETARIAN
PREP 2 HOURS
COOK 20 MINUTES

25g butter, plus extra for
 greasing
75g plain flour
250ml whole milk
150g extra-mature Cheddar,
 grated
415g tin Heinz Beanz
2 tbsp hot sauce (we like
 sriracha)
3 medium free-range eggs
100g panko breadcrumbs
vegetable oil, for frying
sea salt

You will need a 20 x 20cm
brownie tin and a digital
thermometer if you have one.

Melt the butter in a small saucepan over a medium heat. Once melted, whisk in 25g of the flour. Cook, whisking, for 2 minutes, then gradually pour in the milk, whisking all the while and making sure each addition has been smoothly incorporated before adding more.

Once all the milk has been added, let the sauce bubble away for 5 minutes until smooth and thick, whisking occasionally. Add the cheese and whisk until melted, then take the pan off the heat and leave the sauce to cool for 10 minutes.

Lightly grease a 20 x 20cm brownie tin with butter, then line the base and sides with baking paper.

Drain the beans through a sieve, keeping the juice in a small bowl for later, then tip the beans into a large bowl. Add the cooled white sauce and mix together to combine, then spread the mixture into the brownie tin. Cover and put into the freezer for at least 2 hours to set.

Meanwhile, mix the bean juice with the hot sauce – this is going to be your dipping sauce. Set aside.

Crack the eggs into a wide, shallow bowl and whisk until fully combined. Put the remaining flour in a second wide, shallow bowl and put the panko breadcrumbs into a third.

Continued on page 32

CHEESY CROQUETTES
(CONTINUED)

Remove the croquette mixture from the freezer and tip it out on to a chopping board. Remove the baking paper, then slice the mixture into 24 small rectangles. Working in batches, coat each croquette completely in the flour, then the egg and finally the breadcrumbs. Repeat the process so that each one is double-coated, then place the breaded croquettes on to a baking tray.

Preheat the oven to 120°C/100°C fan/gas mark ½ and line a plate with paper towels.

Half-fill a medium saucepan with vegetable oil, then heat until the oil reaches 180°C on a digital thermometer. If you don't have one, you can test the oil temperature by dropping in a panko breadcrumb: it should brown in 20 seconds.

Working in batches, carefully lower the croquettes into the oil. Fry for 2–3 minutes until crisp and deeply golden brown. Remove with a slotted spoon and place on the paper towels to drain, then transfer to a roasting tray and put into the oven to keep warm while you fry the remaining croquettes.

Once all the croquettes are fried, sprinkle with a little sea salt and serve with the dipping sauce.

BEANZ FACTS

In 2012, to celebrate Queen Elizabeth II's Diamond Jubilee, Heinz teamed up with **Fortnum & Mason** to sell limited edition cans featuring the 1952 label.

1.5 million tins of Heinz Beanz are sold in the UK every day – Brits eat the most beans per capita worldwide.

In a bid to encourage young artists, Heinz held its very first national competition in the UK in 1958: a children's colouring contest. Inspired by the classic **'cowboy's breakfast'** of baked beans and bacon, the first prize was a pony – or 200 guineas.

FIVE BEANZ SALAD

VEGAN
PREP 10 MINUTES

1 fat garlic clove, crushed

2 tsp ground cumin

1–2 tsp chilli powder
(depending on how spicy
you like it)

2 tbsp red wine vinegar

zest and juice of 1 lime

2 x 415g tins Heinz Five Beanz

340g tinned sweetcorn,
drained

2 red peppers, finely diced

2 celery stalks, finely diced

large handful of coriander,
roughly chopped (stalks
and all)

salt and pepper

In a large bowl, mix together the garlic, cumin, chilli powder, red wine vinegar, lime zest and juice. Whisk together to create a dressing.

Drain one tin of Five Beanz through a sieve, then add to the bowl, along with the second tin (undrained), and the sweetcorn, pepper, celery and coriander. Give everything a good toss to combine, then season to taste and serve.

BOSTON BEANZ JACKETS

PREP 5 MINUTES
COOK 1 HOUR

4 baking potatoes, scrubbed
4 tsp olive oil
salt and pepper
160g diced pancetta
2 banana shallots, finely diced
1 tsp garlic salt
2 x 415g tins Heinz Beanz
4 bay leaves
1 tbsp treacle
2 tsp Dijon mustard
50g butter

Preheat the oven to 200°C/180°C fan/gas mark 6.

Prick the potatoes all over with a sharp knife, then place them on a roasting tray and rub with 2 teaspoons of the oil. Sprinkle with salt and pepper, and bake for 1 hour until cooked through and crisp.

Meanwhile, heat the remaining 2 teaspoons of oil in a medium saucepan over a medium-high heat. Add the pancetta and shallots. Cook, stirring regularly, for 6-8 minutes until the shallots are soft and golden and the pancetta is crisp.

Stir through the garlic salt and cook for another 30 seconds, then tip in the beans. Give everything a good mix, then reduce the heat to medium. Add the bay leaves, treacle and mustard. Stir to combine, then leave to bubble away for 20 minutes until slightly thickened and rich. Season to taste, then turn off the heat. Reheat once the jacket potatoes are cooked.

Put the jacket potatoes on to four plates and cut each one in half. Dot the butter on top to melt, then fill each jacket potato with the Boston beans and enjoy.

This is extra delicious with your favourite cheese grated on top to serve.

SWEET POTATO JACKETS WITH BEANY SALSA

SERVES 4

VEGAN
PREP 10 MINUTES
COOK 45 MINUTES

4 medium sweet potatoes,
    scrubbed
3 tbsp olive oil
1 tbsp fajita seasoning
salt and pepper

For the beany salsa
200g cherry tomatoes,
    quartered
4 spring onions, finely sliced
415g tin Heinz Five Beanz
2 avocados, finely diced
1 tbsp fajita seasoning
zest and juice of 1 lime

Preheat the oven to 200°C/180°C fan/gas mark 6.

Prick the sweet potatoes all over with a sharp knife. Put them on a roasting tray and drizzle over 1 tablespoon of the oil. Rub in the fajita seasoning and plenty of salt and pepper. Bake for 45 minutes until cooked through and crisp.

Meanwhile, in a bowl, mix together the cherry tomatoes, spring onions, beans, avocados, fajita seasoning and lime zest and juice. Season to taste.

When the sweet potatoes are ready, place each one on a plate and cut in half. Drizzle the remaining oil over the sweet potatoes, then top each one with the beany salsa to serve.

BEANZ MEANZ HEINZ

I n 1967, Maurice Drake created the now legendary slogan 'Beanz Meanz Heinz'. He is said to have come up with it in The Victoria pub in Mornington Crescent, London, over a pint or two of beer! The slogan ran for 22 years, and in 2000 it was unanimously voted the best slogan of all time by a panel from the British advertising industry.

The much-loved slogan returned to UK TV screens in a new advert in 2009, and in 2017, Heinz celebrated 50 years of Beanz Meanz Heinz with a series of personalised and regional label designs celebrating the things people associate with Beanz, including Beanz Means Mumz and Beanz Meanz Smilez!

WHAT DOES BEANZ MEAN TO YOU?

BEANZ MEANZ HEINZ
CELEBRATING 50 GOLDEN YEARZ

BEANZ MEANZ SMILEZ
CELEBRATING 50 GOLDEN YEARZ

MEANZ HEINZ

BEANZ MEANZ GRANZ · BEANZ MEANZ SNACKZ · BEANZ MEANZ COMFORTZ · BEANZ MEANZ RECIPEZ · BEANZ MEANZ LAUGHZ · BEANZ MEANZ NANZ · BEANZ MEANZ CHEEZ · BEANZ MEANZ SPUDZ · BEANZ MEANZ BROZ · BEANZ MEANZ FUELZ

BEANZ MEANZ SKOOLZ · BEANZ MEANZ DINZ · BEANZ MEANZ BANTZ · BEANZ MEANZ COUSINZ · BEANZ MEANZ SMILEZ · BEANZ MEANZ FAMILIEZ · BEANZ MEANZ MUMZ · BEANZ MEANZ FAVEZ · BEANZ MEANZ SISTAZ · BEANZ MEANZ POPZ

BEANZ MEANZ YUMMZ · BEANZ MEANZ GALZ · BEANZ MEANZ HOMEZ · BEANZ MEANZ FRIENDZ · BEANZ MEANZ HEINZ · BEANZ MEANZ MATEZ · BEANZ MEANZ MORNINGZ · BEANZ MEANZ EGGZ · BEANZ MEANZ DADZ · BEANZ MEANZ STUDENTZ

BEANZ MEANZ CHIPZ · BEANZ MEANZ HUGZ · BEANZ MEANZ TINZ · BEANZ MEANZ CAFEZ · BEANZ MEANZ KIDZ · BEANZ MEANZ CHATZ · BEANZ MEANZ PALZ · BEANZ MEANZ SONZ · BEANZ MEANZ LOLZ · BEANZ MEANZ UNCLEZ

BEANZ MEANZ GRAMPZ · BEANZ MEANZ AUNTZ · BEANZ MEANZ STORIEZ · BEANZ MEANZ CHILLZ · BEANZ MEANZ LUNCHEZ · BEANZ MEANZ MEMORIEZ · BEANZ MEANZ SUNDAYZ · BEANZ MEANZ TOASTZ · BEANZ MEANZ BANGERZ · BEANZ MEANZ MEALZ

BEANZ MEANZ TOM

BEANZ MEANZ SARAH

BEANZ MEANZ JAMES

BEANZ MEANZ JACK

BEANZ MEANZ EMILY

BEANZ MEANZ JESS

THE BEANZ PIZZA

The year 1995 was a big one: *Toy Story* was on our screens, Take That were filling the airwaves, and the Sony PlayStation was launched in the US – but the biggest event that year has to be the launch of the Beanz Pizza.

It became a true cult classic, to the extent that in 2019, due to popular demand and to celebrate 150 years of Heinz, the Beanz Pizza made a brief and very exclusive comeback. Just 150 were made, and were available for order on Deliveroo, where they were quickly snapped up by nostalgic fans.

BEANZ PIZZA

VEGETARIAN
PREP 5 MINUTES
COOK 25 MINUTES

400g ready-rolled pizza dough
1 fat garlic clove, crushed
4 tbsp tomato purée
1 tbsp water
415g tin Heinz Beanz
½ tsp dried chilli flakes
½ tsp dried oregano
125g mozzarella, drained and
   torn

Remove the pizza dough from the fridge about 15 minutes before you want to use it. Preheat the oven to 200°C/180°C fan/gas mark 6.

In a bowl, mix together the garlic, tomato purée and water. Add the beans, along with the chilli flakes and oregano, and mix to combine.

Unroll the pizza dough, keeping it on its baking paper, and place on a baking tray. Spread the bean mixture over the pizza base, starting in the centre and leaving a roughly 1cm border around the edges. Scatter over the mozzarella.

Bake in the middle of the oven for 20–25 minutes until the cheese is melted and the dough is puffed up and golden brown. Serve and enjoy.

SATAY SWEET POTATO WITH SPICED SUGAR SNAP PEAS

VEGAN
PREP 15 MINUTES
COOK 35 MINUTES

1 tbsp vegetable oil

thumb-sized piece of fresh ginger, peeled and grated

2 fat garlic cloves, grated

2 tsp ground turmeric

2 tsp ground coriander

2 tsp ground cumin

2 sweet potatoes, peeled and chopped into small chunks

400ml tin coconut milk

2 x 415g tins Heinz Beanz

2 tbsp smooth peanut butter

juice of 1 lime

salt and pepper

4 tsp crispy chilli oil

50g roasted salted peanuts, roughly chopped

handful of fresh coriander, roughly chopped (stalks and all)

For the spiced sugar snap peas

1 tbsp vegetable oil

200g sugar snap peas

1 tsp ground coriander

1 tsp ground cumin

Heat the vegetable oil in a large saucepan over a medium heat. Add the ginger and garlic and cook, stirring, for 30 seconds, then add the turmeric, ground coriander and cumin. Cook, stirring, for 30 seconds more.

Add the sweet potato and stir so it gets coated in all the spices, then add the coconut milk. Refill the coconut milk tin with water and add that too, along with the beans and peanut butter. Give everything a good mix, then leave to bubble away for 25–30 minutes until the sweet potato is completely cooked and the beans are beginning to break down.

Once the sweet potato is nearly cooked, make the spiced sugar snap peas. Heat the oil in a small frying pan over a high heat. Add the sugar snap peas, along with the ground coriander and cumin. Stir-fry for 2 minutes until the peas are just softened. Season with salt and pepper, then take off the heat.

Squeeze the lime juice into the sweet potato satay and season to taste, then divide between four bowls. Top with the sugar snap peas, crispy chilli oil, peanuts and fresh coriander, and serve.

ROASTED SQUASH, SPINACH & FETA FILO PIE

VEGETARIAN
PREP 10 MINUTES
COOK 45 MINUTES

1 large butternut squash, peeled and cut into medium chunks

2 red onions, each cut into 8 wedges

4 tbsp olive oil

2 tbsp cumin seeds

1 tbsp smoked paprika

salt and pepper

500g frozen chopped spinach, defrosted

200g feta, crumbled

415g tin Heinz Beanz

6 sheets of filo pastry

1 tbsp sesame or poppy seeds

You will need a pastry brush.

Preheat the oven to 220°C/200°C fan/gas mark 7.

Tip the squash and onions into a large roasting tin. Drizzle over 2 tablespoons of the olive oil, then scatter over the cumin seeds, paprika and plenty of seasoning. Toss to combine, then roast for 25 minutes until completely soft.

Meanwhile, put the defrosted spinach into a sieve. Holding it over the sink, press out as much water as possible. Tip the spinach into a large bowl, then add the feta and beans. Mix well to combine.

Once the vegetables are roasted, remove the roasting tin from the oven and reduce the heat to 200°C/180°C fan/gas mark 6.

Add the spinach, feta and bean mixture to the roasted squash and onions and stir to combine, then pat the mixture down into an even layer.

Unroll the sheets of filo pastry and brush with the remaining oil. Use clean hands to scrunch up each sheet of pastry, then pile them on top of the bean and vegetable mixture. Repeat until the whole thing is covered, then sprinkle over the sesame or poppy seeds.

Bake the pie for 15–20 minutes until the pastry is crisp and deeply golden. Leave to cool for 5 minutes before serving.

BEANZ ADVENTURE

Baked beans have always been popular with adventurers, as they travel so well. Most of us have probably enjoyed them by the fire at a campsite, but they even made it all the way to Antarctica. Crates of Heinz beans were taken on the ill-fated Terra Nova Expedition, which was captained by Robert F. Scott. Heinz was one of several companies to provide supplies for the 1910–13 expedition, during which Scott and four others died. This photo of one of the team sitting on a crate while tucking into a tin of beans became iconic – and perhaps launched the tradition of enjoying baked beans on camping trips.

SAUSAGE & KALE PASTA BAKE

PREP 15 MINUTES
COOK 45 MINUTES

6 large good-quality pork
    sausages
salt and pepper
1 tbsp olive oil
1 onion, finely chopped
3 fat garlic cloves, crushed
1 tsp dried chilli flakes
2 tsp fennel seeds (optional)
500g passata
2 x 415g tins Heinz Beanz
400g conchiglie (pasta shells)
200g kale
50g Cheddar, grated
50g mozzarella, grated

Preheat the oven to 200°C/180°C fan/gas mark 6.

Squeeze the sausages from their skins into a large bowl. Season with salt and pepper and mix to combine, then use clean hands to roll the mixture into 12 small meatballs.

Heat the oil in a large non-stick frying pan over a medium-high heat. Add the meatballs and fry for 5 minutes until crisp and browned, turning regularly. Transfer to a plate and set aside.

Reduce the heat to medium and add the onion to the pan. Cook, stirring, for 8–10 minutes until softened but not coloured. Add the garlic, chilli flakes and fennel seeds, if using. Cook for 30 seconds, then stir in the passata and beans.

Return the meatballs to the pan. Reduce the heat to low and leave to gently simmer while you cook the pasta.

Bring a large saucepan of salted water to the boil. Drop in the conchiglie and cook for 8 minutes, then drop in the kale and cook for 2 minutes more. Drain both into a colander, shaking off any excess water.

Tip the pasta and kale into the pan of meatballs and sauce. Toss to combine, then spoon into a medium-sized baking dish. Sprinkle over the grated cheese and bake for 15–20 minutes until the top is golden and bubbling. Leave to cool for 5 minutes before tucking in.

GREEN POTATO PIE

VEGETARIAN
PREP 5 MINUTES
COOK 40 MINUTES

500g floury potatoes (we
    like Maris Piper or King
    Edwards), peeled and
    halved
salt and pepper
1 large head of broccoli, cut
    into medium florets and
    stalk roughly chopped
250g frozen peas
2 x 415g tins Heinz Beanz
2 tsp English mustard
a few thyme sprigs, leaves
    picked (optional)
50ml whole milk
50g butter
100g extra-mature Cheddar,
    grated

Preheat the oven to 200°C/180°C fan/gas mark 6.

Put the potatoes in a large saucepan filled with cold salted water. Place over a medium–high heat and bring to the boil. Cook for 10 minutes, then add the broccoli to the pan. Cook for a further 6 minutes, then add the peas and cook for 2 minutes more. By this time, the potatoes and broccoli will be completely tender: a knife should slide into the centre with no resistance. Drain everything into a colander and leave to steam dry.

Tip the beans into a medium-sized roasting tray. Stir through the mustard and thyme, if using, then season well.

Tip the steamed vegetables back into their pan. Add the milk and butter, then use a potato masher to mash well. Stir through most of the grated Cheddar and season to taste.

Spread the green mash over the top of the beans, then use a fork to create some texture in the mash. Scatter over the remaining grated cheese.

Bake the pie for 15–20 minutes until the mash is bubbling and the cheese is melted and golden. Leave to cool for 5 minutes before serving with a big salad.

BEANZ FACTS

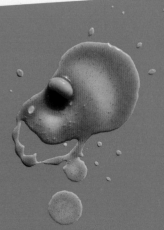

Heinz UK salesmen used to carry a hot flask of beans with them to provide samples to their customers.

The original recipe for Heinz Baked Beans was based on Boston beans and so used to contain pork, but due to wartime shortages in the Second World War, Heinz switched to the vegetarian recipe we know and love today.

The Harlesden factory was bombed twice during the war, but didn't cease production.

HEINZ BAKED BEANS
WITH TOMATO SAUCE.

The beans are actually BAKED, not boiled. The quantity for each can is weighed to insure uniform proportion of beans and sauce. No such flavor found in any other.

SWEET PICKLES,
TOMATO KETCHUP,   TOMATO SOUP,
INDIA RELISH,   PRESERVES,
CELERY SALAD,   TOMATO CHUTNEY,
MUSTARD DRESSING.

Altogether Pure Food **57** Varieties of Products,

Which are distributed everywhere through our Branch Houses.

PRINCIPAL PLANT,—PITTSBURGH, U.S.A.

BREAKFAST BURRITO

VEGETARIAN
PREP 10 MINUTES
COOK 15 MINUTES

50g butter

300g chestnut mushrooms, sliced

2 fat garlic cloves, peeled

1 tbsp ground cumin

6 medium free-range eggs

415g tin Heinz Beanz

4 large tortilla wraps

For the salsa

250g baby plum tomatoes, halved

1 small red onion, finely chopped

6 pickled jalapeño slices, roughly chopped

handful of coriander, roughly chopped (stalks and all)

zest and juice of 1 lime

salt and pepper

First make the salsa. In a bowl, mix together the tomatoes, red onion, pickled jalapeño, coriander, and lime zest and juice. Season to taste, then set aside.

Melt 20g of the butter in a medium non-stick frying pan over a high heat. Add the mushrooms, along with a pinch of salt, and fry for 10 minutes until deeply golden brown and crisp. Crush in the garlic cloves, then add the cumin. Cook, stirring, for 30 seconds more, then tip into a bowl.

Crack the eggs into a jug and whisk well with a fork. Season with plenty of salt and pepper.

Tip the beans into a small saucepan over a medium heat. Cook for 3–4 minutes, stirring occasionally until heated through.

Meanwhile, place the frying pan you used for the mushrooms over a medium heat and add the remaining 30g of butter to melt (no need to wash the pan in between – this gives you extra flavour!). Pour in the beaten egg and cook, stirring every 20 seconds or so until you end up with big pieces of silky scrambled eggs.

Heat the tortilla wraps in the microwave on high for 30 seconds, then assemble the burritos. Divide the scrambled eggs, mushrooms, beans and tomato salsa evenly between the wraps, then roll up each one into a burrito to serve.

CHICKEN ARRABBIATA

PREP 5 MINUTES
COOK 30 MINUTES

2 free-range skinless,
   boneless chicken breasts,
   sliced into 2cm strips
salt and pepper
2 tbsp olive oil
3 fat garlic cloves, finely sliced
1 red chilli, finely sliced
415g tin Heinz Beanz
2 x 400g tins chopped
   tomatoes
1 tbsp balsamic vinegar
400g fresh tagliatelle
handful of basil, leaves picked
50g toasted pine nuts

Season the chicken all over with salt and pepper. Heat 1 tablespoon of the oil in a large frying pan over a high heat. Add the chicken strips and fry, turning regularly, for 5–6 minutes until evenly golden and cooked through. Transfer to a plate.

Reduce the heat to medium and add the remaining 1 tablespoon of oil to the frying pan (no need to wash it first – extra flavour!). Add the garlic and chilli and cook for 1 minute, stirring, until the garlic turns lightly golden. Now tip in the beans and chopped tomatoes. Add the balsamic vinegar, and give everything a good stir, then leave the sauce to bubble away for 15 minutes.

After 15 minutes, reduce the heat to low and return the chicken to the pan to warm through. Season the sauce to taste.

Bring a large saucepan of salted water to the boil. Drop in the fresh tagliatelle and cook according to the packet instructions, then drain and add to the pan with the sauce.

Give everything a good toss to combine, then divide between four bowls. Top with the basil and toasted pine nuts to serve.

LOUISIANA-STYLE BEANS

PREP 10 MINUTES
COOK 35 MINUTES

2 tbsp olive oil

6 spring onions, 5 chopped into 2cm lengths, 1 finely sliced

2 green peppers, finely sliced

2 celery stalks, finely sliced

2 garlic cloves, crushed

2 tbsp Cajun seasoning

2 x 415g tins Heinz Beanz

300ml chicken stock

300g long-grain rice

180g shredded cooked ham hock

salt and pepper

handful of parsley, roughly chopped (stalks and all)

Heat the oil in a large saucepan over a medium heat. Add the chopped spring onions, along with the peppers and celery. Season with a pinch of salt and cook, stirring occasionally, for 8–10 minutes until softened but not browned.

Add the garlic and cook, stirring, for 30 seconds more, then stir in the Cajun seasoning and cook for another 30 seconds. Tip in the beans and chicken stock and bring to a simmer, then leave to bubble away for 20 minutes.

Meanwhile, cook the rice according to the packet instructions.

After the beans have been cooking for 20 minutes, add the ham hock to the pan and stir. Cook for a further 2–3 minutes until the ham is heated through, then season to taste.

Divide the rice between four bowls and spoon over the Louisiana-style beans. Top with the finely sliced spring onion and parsley to serve.

REFRIED BEAN TACOS

VEGAN
PREP 10 MINUTES
COOK 30 MINUTES

1 large butternut squash, skin
　left on, cut into medium
　chunks
1 large cauliflower, cut into
　medium florets and stalk
　roughly chopped
2 tbsp olive oil
2 tbsp cumin seeds
salt and pepper
1 small red onion, very finely
　sliced
juice of 2 limes
2 x 415g tins Heinz Beanz
2–3 tsp chipotle paste
　(depending on how spicy
　you like it)
12 hard-shell tacos
handful of coriander, roughly
　chopped (stalks and all)

Preheat the oven to 220°C/200°C fan/gas mark 7.

Tip the squash and cauliflower on to your largest roasting tray. Drizzle over the olive oil, then scatter over the cumin seeds and plenty of salt and pepper. Toss to combine, then spread out into a single layer so that the veg chunks roast evenly. Roast for 25–30 minutes until the veg is cooked through and a little caramelised.

Meanwhile, in a small bowl, combine the red onion with the juice of 1 lime. Add a big pinch of salt, then use clean hands to scrunch the onion into the lime juice – this will help it soften and quickly pickle. Set aside.

When the vegetables are nearly cooked, tip the beans into a medium saucepan over a medium heat. Cook, stirring occasionally, for 3–4 minutes until warmed through, then add the chipotle paste and remaining lime juice. Using a potato masher, roughly mash the beans, then season to taste.

Heat the tacos according to packet instructions, then assemble. Spoon the chipotle beans into the bottom of each taco, then top with the roasted veg, followed by the quick-pickled onions and coriander. Serve and enjoy.

CREAMY TUSCAN-STYLE SOUP

VEGETARIAN OPTION
PREP 5 MINUTES
COOK 30 MINUTES

1 tbsp olive oil, plus extra to
  serve
2 banana shallots, finely
  chopped
salt and pepper
4 fat garlic cloves, finely
  chopped
a few rosemary sprigs, leaves
  picked and finely chopped
½ tsp dried chilli flakes, plus
  extra to serve
2 x 415g tins Heinz Beanz
1.2 litres chicken or vegetable
  stock
3 bay leaves
150ml double cream
1 tbsp sherry vinegar
rosemary focaccia, to serve

You will need a blender.

Heat the oil in a large saucepan over a medium heat. Add the shallots, along with a pinch of salt, and cook for 8-10 minutes, stirring occasionally, until softened but not coloured.

Add the garlic, along with most of the rosemary and chilli flakes. Cook, stirring, for 1 minute, then add the beans, stock and bay leaves. Reduce the heat to low and leave the soup to bubble away for 10 minutes, then stir through the double cream and vinegar.

Ladle half the soup (minus the bay leaves) into a blender and blitz until smooth. Tip the blitzed soup back into the saucepan and stir to combine with the un-blitzed soup – this is the secret to extra creaminess. Season to taste (we like lots of black pepper) and remove and discard the bay leaves.

Reheat the soup if necessary, then ladle into four bowls. Top each serving with a drizzle of olive oil, along with a scattering of the remaining rosemary and chilli flakes. Serve with the rosemary focaccia.

This soup freezes well in an airtight container. Reheat thoroughly before serving.

SPICED PANEER ROLLS WITH RAITA

VEGETARIAN
PREP 10 MINUTES
COOK 15 MINUTES

100g baby spinach leaves
4 large roti or naan

For the spicy beans
1 tbsp cumin seeds
415g tin Heinz Beanz
2 tsp medium curry powder
1 tbsp mango chutney, plus
    extra to serve

For the raita
½ cucumber
½ green chilli, finely chopped
handful of mint leaves,
    roughly chopped
150g natural yoghurt
salt and pepper

For the crispy paneer
2 tbsp vegetable oil
2 tbsp medium curry powder
450g paneer, cut into large
    cubes

Begin by making the spicy beans. Toast the cumin seeds in a dry saucepan over a medium-high heat for 1 minute until fragrant. Tip half into a small bowl and set aside. Add the beans to the pan with the remaining seeds and reduce the heat to low. Add the curry powder and mango chutney. Mix well and leave to gently cook, stirring occasionally, while you make everything else.

For the raita, finely grate the cucumber into a sieve. Squeeze to remove as much moisture as possible, then tip into the bowl with the reserved toasted cumin seeds. Add the green chilli, mint and yoghurt, and stir. Season, then set aside.

For the paneer, pour the oil into a large bowl. Add the curry powder and cubed paneer, along with some seasoning. Toss well so that each piece of paneer gets coated in the oil and spice mix. Heat a large non-stick frying pan over a high heat and fry the paneer, in two batches, turning regularly, until crisp and browned – this will take around 5 minutes for each batch.

Meanwhile, add half the spinach to the beans and leave to wilt. Heat the roti or naan according to the packet instructions.

To assemble, lay the remaining spinach leaves across the centre of each roti or naan. Top with the beans and crispy paneer, then spoon over the raita and roll up. Serve with more mango chutney.

BEANZ ADVERTS THROUGH THE YEARS

One of the earliest adverts for Heinz Baked Beans, this was created just a year after their launch.

1896

1955

This ad from 1910 sings the praises of Heinz Baked Beans and encourages buyers to 'Try them with your bacon for breakfast; you will then want to eat them for dinner and supper.'

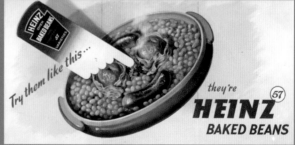

A large outdoor poster from 1955.

1957

A couple of tasty serving ideas can be seen in this ad from 1957.

1962

A playful ad from 1962 celebrating children's love of Heinz Baked Beans.

A classic ad from 1964.

1964

1968

The iconic 'Beanz Meanz Heinz' slogan in all its glory.

1974

This Heinz advert from a 1974 issue of *Good Housekeeping* shares creative ways to cook with beans.

1975

More 70s meal ideas from a 1975 issue of *Family Circle*.

1979

A super sweet poster from 1979.

1981

How to worry kidneys.

Think of chilli con carne and you think of kidney beans. Boring. Now think of chilli con

carne and a tin full of these. Looks harmless? Don't you believe it. That is a Heinz Curried Bean.

Complete with sultanas and a mild curry sauce, a tin of Heinz Curried Beans will scare the pants off any casserole.

Try them. You could have a pleasant surprise.

Heinz Curried Beans. Makes other beans seem half baked.

This 1981 ad in *Good Housekeeping* introduces the reader to the delights of Heinz Curried Beans.

This 1983 ad appeared in *Woman & Home* and shared some of the nutritional benefits of Heinz Baked Beans...

... while this ad from *Woman's Weekly* shows how Heinz Baked Beans can help kids eat their veggies!

A sporty ad from 1986.

Beanz + toast = classic.

OVEN WEDGES WITH BEANZ & FRIED EGGS

SERVES 4

VEGETARIAN
PREP 5 MINUTES
COOK 40 MINUTES

salt and pepper
1kg floury potatoes (we
    like Maris Piper or King
    Edwards), cut into chunky
    wedges, skin left on
1½ tbsp + 1 tsp olive oil
1 tbsp smoked paprika, plus a
    pinch to serve
2 x 415g tins Heinz Beanz
40g butter
4 medium free-range eggs

Preheat the oven to 220°C/200°C fan/gas mark 7.

Bring a large saucepan of salted water to the boil. Once boiling, add the potato wedges and cook for 7 minutes, then drain into a colander and leave to steam dry for a few minutes.

Tip the wedges out on to your largest roasting tray. Drizzle over the 1½ tablespoons of olive oil and sprinkle over the smoked paprika. Season well and toss to combine, then spread into a single layer so that the wedges roast evenly. Roast for 20–25 minutes, flipping halfway, until cooked through, golden and crisp.

When the wedges are nearly ready, tip the beans into a saucepan over a medium heat. Add 20g of the butter and cook for 3–4 minutes, stirring occasionally, until warmed through.

Meanwhile, melt the remaining 20g butter and 1 tsp olive oil in a large non-stick frying pan over a medium-high heat. Crack in the eggs and fry for 2–3 minutes until cooked to your liking.

Divide the wedges, beans and fried eggs between four plates and sprinkle over a little smoked paprika to serve.

If you are not veggie, this would be lovely with a gammon steak.

BEEF ENCHILADAS

PREP 5 MINUTES
COOK 1 HOUR

2 tbsp olive oil
250g good-quality beef mince
salt and pepper
1 onion, finely chopped
1 tbsp ground cumin
2–3 tsp chilli powder
   (depending on how spicy
   you like it)
1 tsp dried oregano
2 x 415g tins Heinz Beanz
2 fat garlic cloves, crushed
500g passata
4 large flour tortillas
50g mozzarella, grated
50g Cheddar, grated
soured cream, to serve

Preheat the oven to 200°C/180°C fan/gas mark 6.

Heat 1 tablespoon of the olive oil in a large frying pan over a high heat. Season the beef with salt and pepper, then stir-fry for 6–8 minutes until crisp and browned. Transfer to a bowl and set aside.

Reduce the heat to medium and add the remaining 1 tablespoon of oil to the pan. Add the onion, along with a pinch of salt. Cook, stirring occasionally, for 8–10 minutes until the onion is softened. Now return the mince to the pan. Stir in the ground cumin, chilli powder and oregano and cook for 1 minute, then add the beans. Stir well, then leave to bubble away for 15 minutes, stirring occasionally.

Meanwhile, in a large bowl, combine the garlic and passata. Season to taste.

Season the beefy beans, then divide them between the tortillas. Fold in the sides, then roll up each tortilla. Spoon half the garlicky passata into the bottom of a medium-sized baking dish, then place the enchiladas on top, side by side. Spoon the remaining passata over the top and scatter over the grated cheese. Bake for 20–25 minutes until the cheese is melted and the enchiladas are bubbling and golden. Serve with soured cream.

For a zesty finish, scatter over freshly chopped coriander before serving.

SMOKED CHEDDAR MELTS

VEGETARIAN
PREP 15 MINUTES
COOK 20 MINUTES

1 medium free-range egg
plain flour, for dusting
500g puff pastry block
200g tin Heinz Beanz
100g smoked Cheddar, grated

You will need a rolling pin and a pastry brush.

Preheat the oven to 200°C/180°C fan/gas mark 6 and line a large baking tray with baking paper.

Crack the egg into a small bowl and whisk well with a fork.

On a lightly floured surface, roll out the pastry into a rectangle measuring roughly 30 x 40cm, about 5mm thick. Cut the rectangle in half and then cut each half into quarters so you are left with eight equally sized rectangles.

Place four of the rectangles on the lined baking tray. Spoon a quarter of the beans into the centre of each, then top with a quarter of the cheese, leaving a 1cm border around the edge.

Brush the beaten egg around the empty borders of pastry, then stick the remaining rectangles of pastry on top to completely encase the beans and cheese. Using a fork, crimp the borders of the pastry to seal, then transfer the pastry pockets to the fridge for 20 minutes to chill.

Brush the remaining egg all over the pastry pockets, then use a small sharp knife to score four diagonal lines across the top of each. Bake in the oven for 15–20 minutes until puffed up and deeply golden. Leave to cool for 5 minutes before tucking in.

BEANZ FACTS

In 1976, **The Who** released their album *Sell Out*. The iconic front cover featured frontman **Roger Daltrey** lying in a bathtub filled with Heinz Baked Beanz.

To celebrate 100 years of Beanzy deliciousness, in 1995 Heinz hid 100 18-carat gold beans in random tins across the UK. Imagine finding one of those on your jacket potato!

The Kitt Green factory
in Wigan stretches over
200,000 square metres
– that's the same size as
27 football pitches. The
factory goes through
140 tonnes of haricot beans
every day, and produces
20 million tins of Heinz Beanz
a week. Queen Elizabeth II
and Prince Philip visited the
factory in 2009 to celebrate
its 50th anniversary. They're
not the first royals to visit,
though – the Queen Mother
also popped over in 1959.

CHIPOTLE CHICKEN CASSEROLE

PREP 5 MINUTES
COOK 30 MINUTES

2 free-range, skin-on chicken
    breasts
salt and pepper
2 tbsp olive oil
1 red onion, finely sliced
1 red pepper, finely sliced
400g tin cherry tomatoes
415g tin Heinz Beanz
2–3 tsp chipotle paste
    (depending on how spicy
    you like it)
200g long-stem broccoli, cut
    into thirds
soured cream and freshly
    chopped coriander, to
    serve

Season the chicken breasts on both sides with salt and pepper. Heat 1 tablespoon of the oil in a large, high-sided frying pan over a medium–high heat. Add the chicken breasts, skin-side down, and fry for 5–6 minutes until the skin is golden and crisp. Transfer the chicken to a plate.

Heat the remaining oil in the frying pan, keeping it over the same heat (no need to wash the pan in between – you want the extra flavour!). Add the onion and pepper. Cook, stirring occasionally, for 5–6 minutes until softened and beginning to colour.

Add the cherry tomatoes to the pan, then half-fill the tin with water and add that too. Stir and then add the beans, chipotle paste and broccoli. Give everything a good stir to combine, then bring the casserole to a simmer.

Return the chicken breasts to the pan, nestling them into the mixture, skin-side up. Let it bubble away for 15 minutes until the chicken is cooked through.

Season the casserole to taste, then bring the pan to the table to serve, along with soured cream and freshly chopped coriander.

BEANZ FALAFEL WRAP

VEGETARIAN
PREP 20 MINUTES
COOK 20 MINUTES

spray oil, for cooking
2 x 415g tins Heinz Beanz
1 medium free-range egg
1 large red onion, half roughly
    chopped and half very
    finely sliced
4 garlic cloves, crushed
handful of parsley (stalks and
    all)
salt and pepper
3 tbsp ras el hanout
200g chickpea flour
½ small red cabbage, very
    finely sliced
2 carrots, peeled and grated
4 tbsp pomegranate seeds
handful of mint leaves
zest and juice of 2 limes
3 tbsp tahini
2 tbsp water
6 large flatbreads, to serve

Preheat the oven to 220°C/200°C fan/gas mark 7. Spray your largest baking tray with oil or line with baking paper.

Drain the beans through a sieve, reserving the juice, then tip the beans into a food processor. Add the egg and the roughly chopped red onion, along with 3 of the crushed garlic cloves and the parsley. Blitz to a smooth paste, then tip into a large bowl. Add ½ teaspoon of salt, along with the ras el hanout and flour. Beat together to combine. The mixture will look quite wet. Using clean hands, shape the mixture into about 24 walnut-sized falafels and place on the prepared tray. Spray with oil, then bake for 15–20 minutes.

In a large bowl, combine the cabbage, carrot, pomegranate seeds and mint leaves with the reserved bean juice. Add the lime zest and the juice of 1 lime. Toss the slaw to combine and season.

In a small bowl, combine the finely sliced red onion with the juice of ½ lime to make a quick pickle.

In another bowl, combine the remaining garlic with the tahini and water. Add the juice of the remaining ½ lime, and whisk. Season to taste.

Once the falafels are baked, heat the flatbreads in the oven, directly on the oven racks, for a minute or so. When everything is ready, place the falafels, wraps, sauce, slaw and pickle on the table so everyone can assemble their own.

BEANZ FACTS

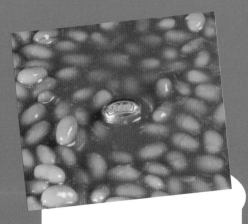

Researchers found that **69%** of Birmingham residents eat baked beans at least once a week – more than anywhere else in the UK – making Brum the Heinz Beanz capital of the world!

In a survey carried out to discover the most unusual places Brits have enjoyed their Beanz, researchers found the most exceptional spots included in a submarine, in a hospital (while in labour!), in a boat on Loch Ness, at the summit of Mount Kilimanjaro and at a Metallica concert. Rock on!

11.5 million Brits have admitted to taking a tin or two of Heinz Beanz on holiday with them.

You might be impressed by the creative uses for beans in the recipes we've shared here, but some of the more adventurous pairings favoured by Beanz enthusiasts include serving Heinz Beanz with chocolate, caviar, ice cream, apple pie, pineapple and custard.

BEANZ CURRY

VEGAN
PREP 5 MINUTES
COOK 30 MINUTES

1 tbsp vegetable oil

1 large red onion, finely
    chopped

salt and pepper

thumb-sized piece of fresh
    ginger, peeled and finely
    chopped

3 fat garlic cloves, finely
    chopped

2 tsp smoked paprika

1 tbsp ground cumin

2 tbsp tomato purée

2 x 415g tins Heinz Beanz

300g basmati rice

100g baby spinach leaves

2 tsp garam masala

handful of coriander, roughly
    chopped

1 lime, cut into 4 wedges

Heat the oil in a large frying pan over a medium heat. Add the onion, along with a pinch of salt, and cook, stirring occasionally, for 8–10 minutes until the onion is softened but not coloured. Add the ginger and garlic and cook, stirring, for 1 minute.

Add the paprika and cumin to the pan and give everything a good stir so that the onion gets coated in the spices. Stir in the tomato purée and cook, stirring, for 1 minute more, then tip in the beans. Give everything a good mix to combine, then leave the curry to simmer away for 15 minutes, stirring occasionally, while you cook the rice according to the packet instructions.

When the rice is ready, add the spinach to the curry and cook until wilted, then stir through the garam masala. Season to taste.

Divide the rice between four bowls. Top with the curry, then scatter over the coriander and serve with the lime wedges.

MEDITERRANEAN ROASTED VEG TRAYBAKE

VEGAN
PREP 10 MINUTES
COOK 40 MINUTES

2 red onions, each cut into
   8 wedges
2 peppers, (we like orange
   and red), cut into medium
   chunks
2 courgettes, cut into medium
   chunks
1 large aubergine, cut into
   medium chunks
3 tbsp olive oil
1 tbsp dried oregano
1-2 tsp dried chilli flakes
   (depending on how spicy
   you like it)
salt and pepper
1 garlic bulb, halved
   horizontally
2 x 415g tins Heinz Beanz
160g mixed pitted olives,
   halved
large handful of basil leaves
50g toasted pine nuts

Preheat the oven to 220°C/200°C fan/gas mark 7.

Tip the onions, peppers, courgettes and aubergine into your largest roasting tin. Drizzle over the oil, then scatter over the oregano, chilli flakes and plenty of seasoning. Toss to combine, then spread out into a single layer so that the veg chunks roast evenly. Nestle in the garlic bulb halves, positioning them cut-side up. Roast for 20–30 minutes, flipping the veg over halfway through, until roasted and completely soft.

Squeeze the garlic cloves from their skins into the vegetables. Tip in the baked beans and olives and stir to combine. Return to the oven for another 10 minutes, then scatter over the basil leaves and pine nuts to serve.

BEANZ FACTS

In 2009, Heinz created a prototype for the world's smallest microwave. The USB powered **'Beanzawave'** was designed to enable office workers to heat up 'snap pots' of Beanz at their desks.

In 2007, Heinz joined in with **Fortnum & Mason's 300th birthday** celebrations by producing a limited edition run of **3,000** tins of Heinz Beanz in the iconic Fortnum & Mason colours.

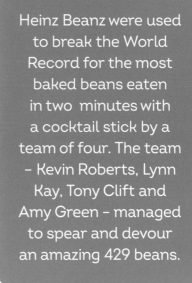

Zoella, Gigi Hadid, Zayn Malik, Ellie Goulding and Joss Stone are all known to be fanz of Heinz Beanz.

Heinz Beanz were used to break the World Record for the most baked beans eaten in two minutes with a cocktail stick by a team of four. The team – Kevin Roberts, Lynn Kay, Tony Clift and Amy Green – managed to spear and devour an amazing 429 beans.

HARISSA FISH PARCELS

PREP 15 MINUTES
COOK 20 MINUTES

2 x 415g tins Heinz Beanz
2 tbsp harissa
salt and pepper
4 x 120g sustainably sourced
    skinless and boneless white
    fish fillets
zest of 1 lemon

For the courgette salad
3 courgettes, peeled into long
    ribbons with a peeler
50g toasted flaked almonds
large handful of parsley,
    roughly chopped (stalks
    and all)
1 tbsp olive oil
juice of 1 lemon

To serve
1 tsp sumac (optional)
170g Greek yoghurt

Preheat the oven to 200°C/180°C fan/gas mark 6. Cut four pieces of baking paper large enough to completely encase the fish fillets in a parcel, then prepare four slightly larger pieces of kitchen foil. Place each piece of baking paper on top of a piece of foil.

In a large bowl, mix together the beans and harissa and season well. Spoon a quarter of the harissa beans into the centre of each piece of baking paper, then place a fish fillet on top of each one. Season the fish, then scatter over the lemon zest. Bring in the edges of the foil and baking paper and pull them over the fish to create a parcel.

Place the parcels on a large roasting tray and roast for 15–20 minutes until the fish is just cooked through – it will flake into large pieces.

Meanwhile, make the courgette salad. In a large bowl, combine the courgette ribbons with the almonds, parsley and olive oil. Squeeze in the lemon juice, then toss the salad together. Season to taste.

When you're ready to serve, stir the sumac through the Greek yoghurt (if using), then spoon the yoghurt on to four plates. Top each dollop of yoghurt with some courgette salad, then serve with the fish parcels.

INDEX

Published in 2022 by Ebury Press an imprint of Ebury Publishing,
20 Vauxhall Bridge Road,
London SW1V 2SA

Ebury Press is part of the Penguin Random House group of companies
whose addresses can be found at global.penguinrandomhouse.com

The HEINZ trademarks are owned by H.J. Heinz Foods UK Limited
and are used under license. © 2022 H.J. Heinz Foods UK Limited

Publishing Director: Elizabeth Bond
Food Photography: Haarala Hamilton
Design: A2 Creative
Food Styling: Sophie Godwin
Food Styling Assistants: Bella Haycraft Mee and Jodie Nixon
Props Styling: Daisy Shayler Webb
Recipe Writer: Sophie Godwin
Project Editor: Tara O'Sullivan
Development: Kraft Heinz New Ventures

www.penguin.co.uk
A CIP catalogue record for this book is available from the British Library
ISBN 9781529148701

Printed and bound in Latvia by Livonia Print SIA

The authorized representative in the EEA is Penguin Random House Ireland,
Morrison Chambers, 32 Nassau Street, Dublin D02 YH68

Penguin Random House is committed to a sustainable future for our business, our readersand our
planet. This book is made from ForestStewardship Council® certified paper.